# Mars

Written by Charlotte Raby
Illustrated by Laszlo Veres

## Collins

# Then

## Mars had rivers

# 2 moons orbit Mars

Mars had rivers

2 moons orbit Mars

# Now

## airbags get the roamer down

# sunset on Mars

airbags get the roamer down

sunset on Mars

# Soon?

a red hover car

# living rooms and airlock

a red hover car

living rooms and airlock

# ❧ Review: After reading ❧

Use your assessment from hearing the children read to choose any GPCs, words or tricky words that need additional practice.

## Read 1: Decoding

- Read the whole book to the children and ask them to follow.
- Turn to page 7 and ask the children to read the words. Can they hear the two different sounds the "s" makes in **sunset** (/s/) and **Mars** (/z/)

## Read 2: Vocabulary

- Go back over the book and discuss the pictures. Encourage children to talk about details that stand out for them. Use a dialogic talk model to expand on their ideas and recast them in full sentences as naturally as possible.
- Work together to expand vocabulary by naming objects in the pictures that children do not know.
- Look together at these words and discuss the meaning of each: **airbags** (*bags filled with air*) **airlock** (*a special airtight room between 2 locked doors*).
- Can the children think of other words that contain "air"? (e.g. *airport, aircraft, airtight, airmail, airbase*)

## Read 3: Comprehension

- Turn to pages 10 and 11, and read the heading: **Soon?**. Why do the children think there is a question mark at the end? (e.g. *because it's not certain that this is how Mars will look soon – but it might do!*) Discuss how the pictures show the artist's ideas about what Mars might be like in the future.
- Use pages 14 and 15 to encourage the children to make connections with what they have seen in the book.
- Flip back through the book. Can the children spot some differences between Mars **Then, Now** and **Soon?**
- Ask the children what they know about space landings.